Lo, soul, seest thou not God's purpose from the first?

WALT WHITMAN

*I want you to get out there and walk—better yet, run!—
on the road God called you to travel.*

THE MESSAGE

LITERARY PORTALS TO PRAYER™

WALT WHITMAN

ILLUMINATED BY

THE**MESSAGE**®

COMPILED AND INTRODUCED BY

Norbert Krapf

NORBERT KRAPF

*for Sonia, in honor of
our love of writing
and the Sandeen,*

*Andy
7/25/2020*

acta

See the dedication

WALT WHITMAN
Illuminated by The Message
Compiled and introduced by Norbert Krapf

Series Editor, Gregory F. Augustine Pierce
Design and typesetting by Harvest Graphics
Cover image © Sylwia Pietruszka, under agreement with Unsplash.

Published by ACTA Publications, 4848 N. Clark St.,
Chicago, IL 60640, (800) 397-2282, actapublications.com

Introduction and compilation copyright © 2017 by Norbert Krapf

Library of Congress Number: 2017950183
ISBN: 978-0-87946-598-8
Printed in the United States of America by Total Printing Systems
Year 30 29 28 27 26 25 24 23 22 21 20 19 18 17
Printing 12 11 10 9 8 7 6 5 4 3 2 First

♻ Text printed on 30% post-consumer recycled paper

CONTENTS

A NOTE FROM THE PUBLISHER / 9

INTRODUCTION / 11

SOURCES / 15

PORTALS TO PRAYER / 16

In fond memory of Ernest Sandeen,
poet and professor whose Notre Dame seminar
led me into the depths of Whitman's poetry.

"Whoever walks a furlong without sympathy
walks to his own funeral drest in his shroud."

"SONG OF MYSELF"

Prayer is sometimes difficult. Perhaps we need spiritual inspiration. Something to reignite our spiritual life. A way to initiate a new and fruitful spiritual direction.

Great literature can do these things: inspire, ignite, and initiate.

Which is why ACTA Publications is publishing a series of "Literary Portals to Prayer." The idea is simple: take insightful passages from great authors whose work has stood the test of time and illuminate each selection with a well-chosen quotation from the Bible on the same theme.

To do this, we use a relatively new translation by Eugene Peterson called *The Message: Catholic/Ecumenical Edition*. It is a fresh, compelling, challenging, and faith-filled translation of the Scriptures from ancient languages into contemporary American English that sounds as if it was written yesterday. *The Message* may be new to you, or you may already know it well, but see if it doesn't illuminate these writings of Walt Whitman in delightful ways.

We publish the books in this series in a size that can easily fit in pocket or purse and find a spot on kitchen table, bed stand, work bench, study desk, or exercise machine. These books are meant to be used in a variety of ways. And we feature a variety of authors so you can find the one or ones that can kick-start your prayer life.

So enjoy these portals to prayer by Walt Whitman illuminated by *The Message*. And look for others in this series, including Louisa May Alcott, Hans Christian Andersen, Jane Austen, Charles Dickens, Elizabeth Gaskell, Herman Melville, William Shakespeare, Edith Wharton, and others. Consider them, if you will, literary *lectio divina*.

Gregory F. Augustine Pierce
President and Publisher
ACTA Publications

REGARDING PRESENTATION OF BIBLICAL PASSAGES
FROM *THE MESSAGE*

Some of *The Message* passages paired with Whitman poems in this book are re-lined as free verse poems in the rhythm and form of Whitman, in an attempt to help the reader enjoy the insights they facilitate.

There are so many Walt Whitmans one is tempted to conclude that many if not most readers claim a different one. After all, near the end of "Song of Myself," Whitman proclaims with no excess modesty, some say, and plenty of twinkle in each eye:

> *Do I contradict myself?*
> *Very well then I contradict myself,*
> *(I am large, I contain multitudes).*

What he means in those three lines could take a whole book to explain, but let us instead consider some of the Walt Whitmans we often hear or read about. Prominent are Walt the literary and cultural nationalist who creates a "new" poetry in spoken American English, the adversary of European literary tradition, the free-verse avant-gardist, the prophetic visionary, the bohemian, the champion of the body and sexual liberation. We know the nature-lover (often on a mystical level), the spokesperson for the common man and woman, the voice of the dispossessed. We recognize the celebrator of the music in the speech of city streets and smallest beauties of rural life and the enthusiastic reviewer of theater and opera. Less talked about is Whitman the devotee of the life of the soul, of the universal Spirit within and beyond all things.

Anyone familiar with the expanding editions of *Leaves of Grass* has seen evidence of all these Whitmans, and more. In revisiting the so-called "deathbed edition" (1891-1892), I have discovered another less celebrated poet. After graduate seminars I taught on his work and selected poems in decades of survey and poetry classes at Long Island University, not far from the historic Birthplace in West Hills, as well as a Whitman seminar in Germany, I have, in my seventies, found another quieter poet engaged in an archetypal spiritual quest. The Walt Whitman at the center of this book brings us along on the spiritual journey of his evolving self. The biblical passages from *The Message*, also in the American vernacular, deepen our appreciation of the presence of a seeker exploring the life of the spirit.

The Whitman who speaks as a joiner of all people and things is conjoined at his spiritual center to Whitman the loner. Walt the loner gives us the most memorable lines and visionary poems, such as the "dark patches" and concluding lines in "Crossing Brooklyn Ferry" and the "outsetting bard" who finds his voice and mission on the Paumanok (Long Island) seashore in confronting the pain of loss in "Out of the Cradle Endlessly Rocking." Related is the grieving lover of the assassinated President Lincoln who descends into the dark recesses of the swamp in "When Lilacs Last in the Dooryard Bloom'd" to hear and "tally" the cry of the kindred hermit thrush. Somewhat different is the man in "Song of Myself" who says he could turn and live with the animals because "They do not make me sick discussing their duty to God." "Logic and sermons never convince," this visionary voice proclaims. "The damp of the night drives deeper into my soul."

In the poems that came of the Civil War, the great "Lilacs"

elegy, the powerful "Drum Taps" cluster, and the shorter late poems, Whitman is more spirit-haunted. Learning that his brother George was among the wounded at Fredericksburg, he travels to Virginia and finds him alive, but the human devastation he describes in *Specimen Days* moves him to become a nurse's aide in tent hospitals. After his stroke and aging, we meet a more prayerful Whitman who looks back and into the beyond. Gone is the buoyant optimism of his and our country's youth; present are sober reflections on final things, the "Invisible World."

As a new father at thirty-seven to an adopted baby girl from Colombia, I taught an undergrad "Proseminar" on Whitman at the University of Freiburg, Germany, in 1981. I would like to describe the reading experience of a young woman in that class. Near the semester's end, to solicit the students' personal response to reading and discussing Whitman's poetry, I distributed a questionnaire. Don't fret over making your English "perfect," I advised. Focus on expressing honestly and clearly your response to reading this distinctly American poet. The last question was: "Has your reaction to Whitman changed since you read him the first time?"

This thoughtful student told me that her reaction to reading Whitman did change. At first, she was excited, perhaps even overstimulated by his poetry, but eventually she "calmed down and was quieter." Why? She was more used to him now, she wrote, had a better understanding of her feelings because reading his poetry enabled her to articulate them better. Whitman's work can be challenging, she admitted, because "He is very personal. He forces you to think about your sense of life and you have to be honest with yourself." This can be troublesome, she admitted. The poignancy of her last two sentences haunts me still: "I'm nineteen years old, maybe it's just the time to really feel the intensity and beauty of life. Sometimes I was afraid that this feeling could get lost in my life, but I think it depends on you and your honesty with yourself."

If we can be as honest about our life goals and yearnings as this young German woman was in describing her relationship with Walt Whitman's poems, we can't fail to be grateful for the spiritual journey the same poet takes us on in this book. As I approach seventy-four, I wish I could experience reading out loud and discussing these fifty yoked passages with readers. I have no doubt—rather a renewed faith—that Walt the spiritual seeker and explorer is out there somewhere waiting for us. As he reassures us at the end of "Song of Myself,"

Failing to fetch me at first keep encouraged,
Missing me one place search another,
I stop somewhere waiting for you.

Norbert Krapf

WALT WHITMAN

SELECTIONS FROM

Leaves of Grass, 1891-1892

ABOUT TO BURST

There was a child went forth every day,
And the first object he'd look upon, that object he became,
And that object became part of him for the day or a certain
    part of the day,
Or for many years or stretching cycles of years.

The early lilacs became part of this child,
And grass and white and red morning-glories, and white
    and red clover, and the song of the phoebe-bird,
And the Third-month lambs and the sow's pink-faint litter,
    and the mare's foal and the cow's calf,
And the noisy brook of the barnyard or by the mire
    of the pond-side,
And the fish suspending themselves so curiously below
    there, and the beautiful curious liquid,
And the water-plants with the graceful flat heads, all
    became part of him.

FROM "THERE WAS A CHILD WENT FORTH"

ABOUT TO BURST

One day I went strolling through the orchard,
*   looking for signs of spring,*
Looking for buds about to burst into flower,
*   anticipating readiness, ripeness.*
Before I knew it my heart was raptured,
*   carried away by lofty thoughts!*

SONG OF SONGS 6:11-12

GOD DECIDED FROM THE OUTSET

A child said *What is the grass?* fetching it to me
    with full hands;
How could I answer the child? I do not know what it is any
    more than he.

I guess it must be the flag of my disposition, out of hopeful
    green stuff woven.

Or I guess it is the handkerchief of the Lord,
A scented gift and remembrancer designedly dropt,
Bearing the owner's name someway in the corners, that we
    may see and remark, and say *Whose?*

Or I guess the grass is itself a child, the produced babe
    of the vegetation.
Or I guess it is a uniform hieroglyphic,

And it means, Sprouting alike in broad zones
    and narrow zones,
Growing among black folks as among white,
Kanuck, Tuckahoe, Congressman, Cuff, I give them
    the same, I receive them the same.

FROM "SONG OF MYSELF"

18

GOD DECIDED FROM THE OUTSET

God knew what he was doing from the very beginning.
He decided from the outset to shape the lives
   of those who love him
   along the same lines as the life of his Son.
The Son stands first in the line of humanity he restored.
We see the original and intended shape of our lives
   there in him.

After God made that decision of what his children
   should be like,
   he followed it up by calling people by name.
After he called them by name, he set them on a solid basis
   with himself.
And then, after getting them established,
   he stayed with them to the end,
   gloriously completing what he had begun.

ROMANS 8:29-30

THE ONE WHO COMES AFTER ME

Poets to come! orators, singers, musicians to come!
Not to-day is to justify me and answer what I am for,
But you, a new brood, native, athletic, continental, greater
    than before known,
Arouse! for you must justify me.

I myself but write one or two indicative words for the future,
I but advance a moment only to wheel and hurry back
    in the darkness.

I am a man who, sauntering along without fully stopping,
    turns a casual look upon you and then averts his face,
Leaving it to you to prove and define it,
Expecting the main things from you.

"POETS TO COME"

THE ONE WHO COMES AFTER ME

The very next day John saw Jesus coming toward him
and yelled out,
"Here he is, God's Passover Lamb!
He forgives the sins of the world!
This is the man I've been talking about,
'the One who comes after me but is really ahead of me.'
I knew nothing about who he was—only this:
that my task has been to get Israel ready
to recognize him as the God-Revealer."

JOHN 1:29-30

CAUTION TO THE WIND

I will not make poems with reference to parts,
But I will make poems, songs, thoughts, with reference
      to ensemble,
And I will not sing with reference to a day, but with
      reference to all days,
And I will not make a poem nor the least part of a poem
      but has reference to the soul,
Because having look'd at the objects of the universe, I find
      there is no one not any particle of one but has
      reference to the soul.

FROM "STARTING FROM PAUMANOK"

CAUTION TO THE WIND

As one psalmist puts it,
 God throws caution to the winds,
 giving to the needy in reckless abandon.
His right-living, right-giving ways
 never run out, never wear out.
This most generous God who gives seed to the farmer
 that becomes bread for your meals
 is more than extravagant with you.
He gives you something you can then give away,
 which grows into full-formed lives,
 robust in God, wealthy in every way,
 so that you can be generous in every way,
 producing with us great praise to God.

2 CORINTHIANS 9:9-11

RIGHT HERE AND NOW

As I ebb'd with the ocean of life,
As I wended the shores I know,
As I walk'd where the ripples continually wash
    you Paumanok,*
Where they rustle up hoarse and sibilant,
Where the fierce old mother endlessly cries for her castaways,
I musing late in the autumn day, gazing off southward,
Held by this electric self out of the pride of which I
    utter poems,
Was seiz'd by the spirit that trails in the lines underfoot,
The rim, the sediment that stands for all the water and all
    the land of the globe.

"AS I EBB'D WITH THE OCEAN OF LIFE"

*Paumanok is the Algonquin word for Long Island.

RIGHT HERE AND NOW

This commandment that I'm commanding you today
    isn't too much for you,
    it's not out of your reach.
It's not on a high mountain—
    you don't have to get mountaineers to climb the peak
    and bring it down to your level
    and explain it before you can live it.
And it's not across the ocean—
    you don't have to send sailors out
    to get it, bring it back,
    and then explain it before you can live it.
No. The word is right here and now—
    as near as the tongue in your mouth,
    as near as the heart in your chest.
Just do it!

DEUTERONOMY 30:11-14

PROPERLY FIXED AND FIT TOGETHER

I have said that the soul is not more than the body,
And I have said that the body is not more than the soul,
And nothing, not God, is greater than one's self is,
And whoever walks a furlong without sympathy walks to his
    own funeral drest in his shroud,
And I or you pocketless of a dime may purchase the pick
    of the earth,
And to glance with an eye or show a bean in its pod
    confounds the learning of all times,
And there is no trade or employment but the young man
    following it may become a hero,
And there is no object so soft but it makes a hub for the
    wheel'd universe,
And I say to any man or woman, Let your soul stand cool
    and composed before a million universes.

FROM "SONG OF MYSELF"

PROPERLY FIXED AND FIT TOGETHER

Jesus was supreme in the beginning and
>*—leading the resurrection parade—*
>*he is supreme in the end.*
From beginning to end he's there,
>*towering far above everything,*
>*everyone.*
So spacious is he, so roomy,
>*that everything of God*
>*finds its proper place in him*
>*without crowding.*
Not only that,
>*but all the broken*
>*and dislocated pieces*
>*of the universe*
>*—people and things, animals and atoms—*
>*get properly fixed and fit together*
>*in vibrant harmonies.*

COLOSSIANS 1:18-20

THE GOD-CREATED

In the faces of men and women I see God, and in my own
      face in the glass,
I find letters from God dropt in the street, and every one is
      sign'd by God's name,
And I leave them where they are, for I know that
      whereso'er I go,
Others will punctually come for ever and ever.

FROM "SONG OF MYSELF"

THE GOD-CREATED

Starting from scratch, God made the entire human race
and made the earth hospitable,
with plenty of time and space for living
so we could seek after God,
and not just grope around in the dark
but actually find him.
God doesn't play hide-and-seek with us.
He's not remote; he's near.
We live and move in him,
can't get away from him!
One of your poets said it well:
"We're the God-created."

ACTS 17:26-28

DON'T FEAR THE JUDGMENT OF DEATH

And I say to mankind, Be not curious about God,
For I who am curious about each am not curious about God,
(No array of terms can say how much I am at peace about
    God and about death.)

I hear and behold God in every object, yet understand God
    not in the least,
Nor do I understand who there can be more wonderful
    than myself.

FROM "SONG OF MYSELF"

DON'T FEAR THE JUDGMENT OF DEATH

Don't fear the judgment of death.
   It has embraced everyone
   who went before us
   and will claim everyone
   who comes after us.
Death is the judgment from God
   on every single human being:
   why would we want
   to resist the Most High?
No matter how old we are
   —ten, one hundred, one thousand—
   when we die it's because
   we have no further business on earth,

SIRACH 41:5-8

WHO GETS THE LAST WORD

And as to you Corpse I think you are good manure, but
    that does not offend me,
I smell the white roses sweet-scented and growing,
I reach to the leafy lips, I reach to the polish'd breasts of
    melons.

And as to you Life I reckon you are the leavings
    of many deaths,
(No doubt I have died myself ten thousand times before.)

FROM "SONG OF MYSELF"

WHO GETS THE LAST WORD

In the resurrection scheme of things,
    this has to happen:
    everything perishable taken off the shelves
    and replaced by the imperishable,
    this mortal replaced by the immortal.
Then the saying will come true:
    Death swallowed by triumphant Life!
    Who got the last word, oh, Death?
    Oh, Death, who's afraid of you now?

I CORINTHIANS 15:54-55

MAKING EVERYTHING NEW AGAIN

There was never any more inception than there is now,
Nor any more youth or age than there is now,
And will never be any more perfection than there is now,
Nor any more heaven or hell than there is now.

FROM "SONG OF MYSELF"

MAKING EVERYTHING NEW AGAIN

I heard a voice thunder from the Throne:
  "Look! Look!
  God has moved into the neighborhood,
  making his home with men and women!
  They're his people, he's their God.
  He'll wipe every tear from their eyes.
  Death is gone for good
  —tears gone, crying gone, pain gone—
  all the first order of things gone."

The Enthroned continued:
  "Look!
  I'm making everything new.
  Write it all down—
  each word dependable and accurate."

REVELATION 21:3-5

YOU WON'T SEE MY FACE

I believe in you my soul, the other I am must not abase
    itself to you,
And you must not be abased to the other.

Loafe with me on the grass, loose the stop from your throat,
Not words, not music or rhyme I want, not custom or
    lecture, not even the best,
Only the lull I like, the hum of your valvèd voice.

FROM "SONG OF MYSELF"

YOU WON'T SEE MY FACE

GOD *said,*

> *"Look, here is a place right beside me.*
> *Put yourself on this rock.*
> *When my Glory passes by,*
> *I'll put you in the cleft of the rock*
> *and cover you with my hand*
> *until I've passed by.*
> *Then I'll take my hand away*
> *and you'll see my back.*
> *But you won't see my face."*

EXODUS 33:21-23

HONEST AND TRUE

Has any one supposed it lucky to be born?
I hasten to inform him or her it is just as lucky to die,
    and I know it.

I pass death with the dying and birth with the new-wash'd
    babe, and am not contain'd between my hat and boots,
And peruse manifold objects, no two alike and every
    one good,
The earth good and the stars good, and the adjuncts
    all good.

I am not an earth nor an adjunct of an earth,
I am the mate and companion of people, all just as
    immortal and fathomless as myself,
(They do not know how immortal, but I know.)

FROM "SONG OF MYSELF"

HONEST AND TRUE

I give thanks to GOD with everything I've got—
Wherever good people gather,
and in the congregation.
GOD's works are so great,
worth a lifetime of study
—endless enjoyment!
Splendor and beauty mark his craft;
His generosity never gives out.
His miracles are his memorial—
This GOD of Grace, this GOD of Love....

He manufactures truth and justice;
All his products are guaranteed to last—
Never out-of-date, never obsolete, rust-proof.
All that he makes and does
is honest and true.

PSALM 111:1-4, 7-8

KNOCKING TYRANTS OFF HIGH HORSES

Through me many long dumb voices,
Voices of the interminable generations of prisoners
    and slaves,
Voices of the diseas'd and despairing and of thieves
    and dwarfs,
Voices of cycles or preparation and accretion,
And of the threads that connect the stars, and of wombs
    and of the father-stuff,
And of the rights of them the others are down upon,
Of the deform'd, trivial, flat, foolish, despised,
Fog in the air, beetles rolling balls of dung.

FROM "SONG OF MYSELF"

KNOCKING TYRANTS OFF HIGH HORSES

And Mary said,
I'm bursting with God-news;
    I'm dancing the song of my Savior God.
God took one good look at me, and look what happened—
    I'm the most fortunate woman on earth!
What God has done for me will never be forgotten,
    the God whose very name is holy,
    set apart from all others.
His mercy flows in wave after wave
    on those who are in awe before him.
He bared his arm and showed his strength,
    scattered the bluffing braggarts.
He knocked tyrants off their high horses,
    pulled victims out of the mud.
The starving poor sat down to a banquet;
    the callous rich were left out in the cold.
He embraced his chosen child, Israel;
    he remembered and piled on the mercies,
    piled them high.
It's exactly what he promised,
    beginning with Abraham and right up to now.

LUKE 1:46-55

COME TO ME

Urge and urge and urge,
Always the procreant urge of the world.

Out of the dimness opposite equals advance, always
      substance and increase, always sex,
Always a knit of identity, always distinction, always a breed
      of life.

To elaborate is no avail, learn'd and unlearn'd feel that it is so.

Sure as the most certain sure, plumb in the uprights, well
      entretied, braced in the beams,
Stout as a horse, affectionate, haughty, electrical,
I and this mystery here we stand.

FROM "SONG OF MYSELF"

COME TO ME

Get up, my dear friend,
    fair and beautiful lover—come to me!
Look around you: Winter is over;
    the winter rains are over, gone!
Spring flowers are in blossom all over.
    The whole world's a choir—and singing!
Spring warblers are filling the forest
    with sweet arpeggios.
Lilacs are exuberantly purple and perfumed,
    and cherry trees fragrant with blossoms.
Oh, get up, dear friend,
    my fair and beautiful lover—come to me!
Come, my shy and modest dove—
    leave your seclusion, come out in the open.
Let me see your face,
    let me hear your voice.
For your voice is soothing
    and your face is ravishing.

SONG OF SONGS 2:10-14

OUT OF THE DARKNESS

Logic and sermons never convince,
The damp of the night drives deeper into my soul.

FROM "SONG OF MYSELF"

OUT OF THE DARKNESS

Everything was created through him;
nothing—not one thing!—
came into being without him.
What came into existence was Life,
and the Life was Light to live by.
The Life-Light blazed out of the darkness;
the darkness couldn't put it out.

JOHN 1:3-5

TAKE A GOOD LOOK

I believe a leaf of grass is no less than the journey-work
    of the stars,
And the pismire* is equally perfect, and a grain of sand,
    and the egg of the wren,
And the tree-toad is a chef-d'oeuvre for the highest,
And the running blackberry would adorn the parlors of
    heaven,
And the narrowest hinge in my hand puts to scorn
    all machinery,
And the cow crunching with depress'd head surpasses
    my statue,
And a mouse is miracle enough to stagger sextillions
    of infidels.

FROM "SONG OF MYSELF"

*Ant

TAKE A GOOD LOOK

Take a good look at God's work.
Who could simplify and reduce
        Creation's curves and angles
To a plain straight line?

ECCLESIASTES 7:13

ASK THE ANIMALS

I think I could turn and live with animals, they are so placid
    and self-contain'd,
I stand and look at them long and long.

They do not sweat and whine about their condition,
They do not lie awake in the dark and weep for their sins,
They do not make me sick discussing their duty to God,
Not one is dissatisfied, not one is demented with the mania
    of owning things,
Not one kneels to another, nor to his kind that lived
    thousands of years ago,
Not one is respectable or unhappy over the whole earth.

FROM "SONG OF MYSELF"

ASK THE ANIMALS

Job answered....
"But ask the animals what they think—let them teach you;
let the birds tell you what's going on.
Put your ear to the earth—learn the basics.
Listen—the fish in the ocean will tell you their stories.
Isn't it clear that they all know and agree
that GOD *is sovereign,*
that he holds all things in his hand—
Every living soul, yes,
every breathing creature?
Isn't this all just common sense,
as common as the sense of taste?"

JOB 12:7-11

THERE IT IS

I tramp a perpetual journey, (come listen all!)
My signs are a rain-proof coat, good shoes, and a staff cut
    from the woods,
No friend of mine takes his ease in my chair,
I have no chair, no church, no philosophy,
I lead no man to a dinner-table, library, exchange,
But each man and each woman of you I lead upon a knoll,
My left hand hooking you round the waist,
My right hand pointing to landscapes of continents and
    the public road.

Not I, not any one else can travel the road for you,
You must travel it for yourself.

FROM "SONG OF MYSELF"

THERE IT IS

Moses climbed from the Plains of Moab to Mount Nebo, the peak of Pisgah facing Jericho. God showed him all the land from Gilead to Dan, all Naphtali, Ephraim, and Manasseh; all Judah reaching to the Mediterranean Sea; the Negev and the plains which encircle Jericho, City of Palms, as far south as Zoar.

Then and there GOD said to him,
*   "This is the land I promised to your ancestors,*
*   to Abraham, Isaac, and Jacob*
*   with the words*
*   'I will give it to your descendants.'*
*   I've let you see it with your own eyes.*
*   There it is.*
*   But you're not going to go in."*

DEUTERONOMY 34:1-4

THE FUNDAMENTAL FACT OF EXISTENCE

I do not despise you priests, all time, the world over,
My faith is the greatest of faiths and the least of faiths,
Enclosing worship ancient and modern and all between
    ancient and modern,
Believing I shall come again upon the earth after five
    thousand years,
Waiting responses from oracles, honoring the gods,
    saluting the sun....

FROM "SONG OF MYSELF"

THE FUNDAMENTAL FACT OF EXISTENCE

The fundamental fact of existence
    is that this trust in God,
    this faith,
    is the firm foundation
    under everything that makes life worth living.
    It's our handle on what we can't see.
The act of faith is what distinguished our ancestors,
    set them above the crowd.
By faith,
    we see the world called into existence by God's word,
    what we see created by what we don't see.

HEBREWS 11:1-3

YOU'RE WITH ME ALL THE TIME

I heard you solemn-sweet pipes of the organ as last Sunday
    morn I pass'd the church,
Winds of autumn, as I walk'd the woods at dusk I heard
    your long-stretch'd sighs up above so mournful,
I heard the perfect Italian tenor singing at the opera, I
    heard the soprano in the midst of the quartet singing;
Heart of my love! you too I heard murmuring low through
    one of the wrists around my head,
Heard the pulse of you when all was still ringing little bells
    last night under my ear.

"I HEARD YOU SOLEMN-SWEET PIPES OF THE ORGAN"

YOU'RE WITH ME ALL THE TIME

"All this time his older son was out in the field. When the day's work was done he came in. As he approached the house, he heard the music and dancing. Calling over one of the houseboys, he asked what was going on. He told him, 'Your brother came home. Your father has ordered a feast—barbecued beef!—because he has him home safe and sound.'

"The older brother stalked off in an angry sulk and refused to join in. His father came out and tried to talk to him, but he wouldn't listen. The son said, 'Look how many years I've stayed here serving you, never giving you one moment of grief, but have you ever thrown a party for me and my friends? Then this son of yours who has thrown away your money on whores shows up and you go all out with a feast!'

"His father said, 'Son, you don't understand. You're with me all the time, and everything that is mine is yours—but this is a wonderful time, and we had to celebrate. This brother of yours was dead, and he's alive! He was lost, and he's found!'"

LUKE 15:25-32

"THE PEOPLE I HAVE BLESSED"

The impalpable sustenance of me from all things at all hours
    of the day,
The simple, compact, well-join'd scheme, myself
      disintegrated, everyone disintegrated yet part
      of the scheme,
The similitudes of the past and those of the future,
The glories strung like beads on my smallest sights and
      hearings, on the walk in the street and the passage over
      the river,
The current rushing so swiftly and swimming with me
    far away,
The others that are to follow me, the ties between me
    and them,
The certainty of others, the life, love, sight, hearing of others.

FROM "CROSSING BROOKLYN FERRY"

"THE PEOPLE I HAVE BLESSED"

"Because I, GOD, love fair dealing
    and hate thievery and crime,
I'll pay your wages on time and in full,
    and establish my eternal covenant with you.
Your descendants will become well-known all over.
    Your children in foreign countries
Will be recognized at once
    as the people I have blessed."

ISAIAH 61:8-9

ONE RESCUED LIFE

It is not upon you alone that the dark patches fall,
The dark threw its patches down upon me also,
The best I had done seem'd to me blank and suspicious,
My great thoughts as I supposed them were they not in
    reality meagre?
Nor is it you alone who know what it is to be evil,
I am he who knew what it was to be evil,
I too knitted the old knot of contrariety,
Blabb'd, blush'd, resented, lied, stole, grudg'd,
Had guile, anger, lust, hot wishes I dared not speak,
Was wayward, vain, greedy, shallow, sly, cowardly, malignant,
The wolf, the snake, the hog, not wanting in me,
The cheating look, the frivilous word, the adulterous wish,
    not wanting,
Refusals, hates, postponements, meanness, laziness, none of
    these wanting....

FROM "CROSSING BROOKLYN FERRY"

ONE RESCUED LIFE

By this time a lot of men and women of doubtful reputation were hanging around Jesus, listening intently. The Pharisees and religion scholars were not pleased, not at all pleased. They growled, "He takes in sinners and eats meals with them, treating them like old friends." Their grumbling triggered this story.

"Suppose one of you had a hundred sheep and lost one. Wouldn't you leave the ninety-nine in the wilderness and go after the lost one until you found it? When found, you can be sure you would put it across your shoulders, rejoicing, and when you got home call in your friends and neighbors, saying, 'Celebrate with me! I've found my lost sheep!' Count on it—there's more joy in heaven over one sinner's rescued life than over ninety-nine good people in no need of rescue."

LUKE 15:1-7

MESSAGES OF JOY

You have waited, you always wait, you dumb,
    beautiful ministers,
We receive you with free sense at last, and are insatiate
    henceforward,
Not you any more shall be able to foil us, or withold
    yourselves from us,
We use you, and do not cast you aside—we plant you
    permanently within us,
We fathom you not—we love you—there is perfection
    in you also,
You furnish your parts toward eternity,
Great or small, you furnish your parts toward the soul.

FROM "CROSSING BROOKLYN FERRY"

MESSAGES OF JOY

The Spirit of GOD, the Master, is on me
    because GOD anointed me.
He sent me to preach good news to the poor,
    heal the heartbroken,
    announce freedom to all captives,
    pardon all prisoners.
GOD sent me to announce the year of his grace
    —a celebration of God's destruction of our enemies—
    and to comfort all who mourn,
    to care for the needs of all who mourn in Zion,
    give them bouquets of roses instead of ashes,
    messages of joy instead of news of doom,
    a praising heart instead of a languid spirit.

ISAIAH 61:1-3

"SEND ME!"

Demon or bird! (said the boy's soul,)
Is it indeed toward your mate you sing? or is it really to me?
For I, that was a child, my tongue's use sleeping, now I
      have heard you,
Now in a moment I know what I am for, I awake,
And already a thousand singers, a thousand songs, clearer,
      louder and more sorrowful than yours,
A thousand warbling echoes have started to life within me,
      never to die.

O you singer solitary, singing by yourself, projecting me,
O solitary me listening, never more shall I cease
      perpetuating you,
Never more shall I escape, never more the reverberations,
Never more the cries of unsatisfied love be absent from me,
Never again leave me to be the peaceful child I was before
      what there in the night,
By the sea under the yellow and sagging moon,
The messenger there arous'd, the fire, the sweet hell within,
The unknown want, the destiny of me.

FROM "OUT OF THE CRADLE ENDLESSLY ROCKING"

"SEND ME!"

Then one of the angel-seraphs flew to me. He held a live coal that he had taken with tongs from the altar. He touched my mouth with the coal and said:

"Look. This coal has touched your lips.
    Gone your guilt,
    your sins wiped out."
And then I heard the voice of the Master:
    "Whom shall I send?
    Who will go for us?"
I spoke up,
    "I'll go.
    Send me!"

ISAIAH 6:6-8

TUCKED IN SAFELY AT NIGHT

When I heard the learn'd astronomer,
When the proofs, the figures, were ranged in columns
    before me,
When I was shown the charts and diagrams, to add, divide,
    and measure them,
When I sitting heard the astronomer where he lectured with
    much applause in the lecture-room,
How soon unaccountable I became tired and sick,
Till rising and gliding out I wander'd off by myself,
In the mystical moist night-air, and from time to time,
Look'd up in perfect silence at the stars.

    "WHEN I HEARD THE LEARN'D ASTRONOMER"

TUCKED IN SAFELY AT NIGHT

GOD *answered Job from the eye of a violent storm. He said:*

"Why do you confuse the issue?
    Why do you talk
    without knowing what you're talking about?
Pull yourself together, Job!
    Up on your feet! Stand tall!
I have some questions for you,
    and I want some straight answers.
Where were you when I created the earth?
    Tell me, since you know so much!
Who decided on its size?
    Certainly you'll know that!
Who came up with the blueprints
    and measurements?
How was its foundation poured,
    and who set the cornerstone,
    while the morning stars sang in chorus
    and all the angels shouted praise?
And who took charge of the ocean
    when it gushed forth like a baby from the womb?
That was me! I wrapped it in soft clouds,
    and tucked it in safely at night."

JOB 38:1-11

THE SOUNDS OF PROMISE

I see in you the estuary that enlarges and spreads itself
grandly as it pours in the great sea.

"TO OLD AGE"

THE SOUNDS OF PROMISE

My ears are filled with the sounds of promise:
    "Good people will prosper like palm trees,
Grow tall like Lebanon cedars;
    transplanted to GOD's courtyard,
They'll grow tall in the presence of God,
    lithe and green, virile still in old age."
Such witnesses to upright GOD!
    My Mountain, my huge, holy Mountain!

PSALM 92:12-15

THE FACE OF CHRIST

A sight in camp in the daybreak gray and dim,
As from my tent I emerge so early sleepless,
As slow I walk in the cool fresh air the path near by
    the hospital tent,
Three forms I see on stretchers lying, brought out there
    untended lying,
Over each the blanket spread, ample brownish
    woolen blanket,
Gray and heavy blanket, folding, covering all.

Curious I halt and silent stand,
Then with light fingers I from the face of the nearest the
    first just lift the blanket;
Who are you elderly man so gaunt and grim, with well-
    gray'd hair, and flesh all sunken about the eyes?
Who are you my dear comrade?

Then to the second I step—and who are you my child
    and darling?
Who are you sweet bow with cheeks yet blooming?

Then to the third—a face nor child nor old, very calm, as of
    beautiful yellow-white ivory;
Young man I think I know you—I think this face is the face
    of the Christ himself,
Dead and divine and brother of all, and here again he lies.

"A SIGHT IN THE CAMP IN THE DAYBREAK GRAY AND DIM"

THE FACE OF CHRIST

Remember, our Message is not about ourselves;
    we're proclaiming Jesus Christ,
    the Master.
All we are is messengers,
    errand runners from Jesus for you.
It started when God said,
    "Light up the darkness!"
    and our lives filled up with light
    as we saw and understood God
    in the face of Christ,
    all bright and beautiful.

2 CORINTHIANS 4:5-6

LOVE YOUR ENEMIES

Word over all, beautiful as the sky,
Beautiful that war and all its deeds of carnage must in time
      be utterly lost,
That the hands of the sisters Death and Night incessantly
      softly wash again, and ever again, this soil'd world;
For my enemy is dead, a man divine as myself is dead,
I look where he lies white-faced and still in the coffin—
      I draw near,
Bend down and touch lightly with my lips the white face in
      the coffin.

"RECONCILIATION"

LOVE YOUR ENEMIES

"You're familiar with the old written law, 'Love your friend,' and its unwritten companion, 'Hate your enemy.' I'm challenging that. I'm telling you to love your enemies. Let them bring out the best in you, not the worst. When someone gives you a hard time, respond with the energies of prayer, for then you are working out of your true selves, your God-created selves. This is what God does. He gives his best—the sun to warm and the rain to nourish—to everyone, regardless: the good and bad, the nice and nasty. If all you do is love the lovable, do you expect a bonus? Anybody can do that. If you simply say hello to those who greet you, do you expect a medal? Any run-of-the-mill sinner does that.

"In a word, what I'm saying is, Grow up. You're kingdom subjects. Now live like it. Live out your God-created identity. Live generously and graciously toward others, the way God lives toward you."

MATTHEW 5:43-48

YOU CAN PRAY VERY SIMPLY

Give me the splendid silent sun with all his beams
    full-dazzling,
Give me juicy autumnal fruit ripe and red from the orchard,
Give me a field where the unmow'd grass grows,
Give me an arbor, give me the trellis'd grape,
Give me fresh corn and wheat, give me serene-moving
    animals teaching content,
Give me nights perfectly quiet as on high plateaus west of
    the Mississippi, and I looking up at the stars,
Give me odorous at sunrise a garden of beautiful flowers
    where I can walk undisturb'd,
Give me for marriage a sweet-breath'd woman of whom I
    should never tire,
Give me a perfect child, give me away aside from the noise
    of the world a rural domestic life,
Give me to warble spontaneous songs recluse by myself, for
    my own ears only,
Give me solitude, give me Nature, give me again O Nature
    your primal sanities!

FROM "GIVE ME THE SPLENDID SILENT SUN"

YOU CAN PRAY VERY SIMPLY

"The world is full of so-called prayer warriors who are prayer-ignorant. They're full of formulas and programs and advice, peddling techniques for getting what you want from God. Don't fall for that nonsense. This is your Father you are dealing with, and he knows better than you what you need. With a God like this loving you, you can pray very simply. Like this:

> *"Our Father in heaven,*
> *Reveal who you are.*
> *Set the world right;*
> *Do what's best—*
> > *as above, so below.*
> *Keep us alive with three square meals.*
> *Keep us forgiven with you and forgiving others.*
> *Keep us safe from ourselves and the Devil.*
> *You're in charge!*
> *You can do anything you want!*
> *You're ablaze in beauty!*
> > *Yes. Yes. Yes."*

MATTHEW 6:7-13

DAYS OF GRIEVING ARE OVER

Look down fair moon and bathe this scene,
Pour softly down night's nimbus floods on faces ghastly,
    swollen, purple,
On the dead on their backs with arms toss'd wide,
Pour down your unstinted nimbus sacred moon.

"LOOK DOWN FAIR MOON"

DAYS OF GRIEVING ARE OVER

I'll install Peace to run your country,
  make Righteousness your boss.
There'll be no more stories of crime in your land,
  no more robberies, no more vandalism.
You'll name your main street Salvation Way,
  and install Praise Park at the center of town.
You'll have no more need of the sun by day
  nor the brightness of the moon at night.
GOD will be your eternal light,
  your God will bathe you in splendor.
Your sun will never go down,
  your moon will never fade.
I will be your eternal light.
  Your days of grieving are over.

ISAIAH 60:17-20

"WHY HAVE YOU ABANDONED ME?"

I saw battle-corpses, myriads of them,
And the white skeletons of young men, I saw them,
I saw the debris and debris of all the slain soldiers of the war,
But I saw they were not as was thought,
They themselves were fully at rest, they suffer'd not,
The living remain'd and suffer'd, the mother suffer'd,
And the wife and the child and the musing comrade suffer'd,
And the armies that remain'd suffer'd.

FROM "WHEN LILACS LAST IN THE DOORYARD BLOOM'D"

"WHY HAVE YOU ABANDONED ME?"

At noon the sky became extremely dark. The darkness lasted three hours. At three o'clock, Jesus groaned out of the depths, crying loudly, "Eloi, Eloi, lama sabachthani?" which means, "My God, my God, why have you abandoned me?"

MARK 15:33-34

FOLLOW ME

From deep secluded recesses,
From the fragrant cedars and the ghostly pines so still,
Came the carol of the bird.

And the charm of the carol rapt me,
As I held as if by their hands my comrades in the night,
And the voice of my spirit tallied the song of the bird.

Come lovely and soothing death,
Undulate round the world, serenely arriving, arriving,
In the day, in the night, to all, to each,
Sooner or later delicate death.

Prais'd be the fathomless universe,
For life and joy, and for objects and knowledge curious,
And for love, sweet love—but praise! praise! praise!
For the sure-enwinding arms of cool-enfolding death.

FROM "WHEN LILACS LAST IN THE DOORYARD BLOOM'D"

FOLLOW ME

Then Jesus said it a third time: "Simon, son of John, do you love me?"

Peter was upset that he asked for the third time, "Do you love me?" so he answered, "Master, you know everything there is to know. You've got to know that I love you."

Jesus said, "Feed my sheep. I'm telling you the very truth now: When you were young you dressed yourself and went wherever you wished, but when you get old you'll have to stretch out your hands while someone else dresses you and takes you where you don't want to go." He said this to hint at the kind of death by which Peter would glorify God. And then he commanded, "Follow me."

JOHN 21:17-19

YOUR HEAD WILL SWIM

Now I am terrified at the Earth, it is that calm and patient,
It grows such sweet things out of such corruptions,
It turns harmless and stainless on its axis, with such endless
    successions of diseas'd corpses,
It distills such exquisite winds out of such infused fetor,
It renews with such unwitting looks its prodigal, annual,
    sumptuous crops,
It gives such divine materials to men, and accepts such
    leavings from them at last.

FROM "THIS COMPOST"

YOUR HEAD WILL SWIM

"*Yes indeed, it won't be long now.*" GOD's Decree.

"*Things are going to happen so fast your head will swim, one thing fast on the heels of the other. You won't be able to keep up. Everything will be happening at once—and everywhere you look, blessings! Blessings like wine pouring off the mountains and hills. I'll make everything right again for my people Israel:*

"*They'll rebuild their ruined cities.*
They'll plant vineyards and drink good wine.
They'll work their gardens and eat fresh vegetables.
And I'll plant them, *plant them on their own land.*
They'll never again be uprooted
from the land I've given them."
GOD, your God, says so.

AMOS 9:13-15

A SPIDER WEB

A noiseless patient spider,
I mark'd where on a little promontory it stood isolated,
Mark'd how to explore the vacant vast surrounding,
It launch'd forth filament, filament, filament, out of itself,
Ever unreeling them, ever tirelessly speeding them.

And you O my soul where you stand,
Surrounded, detached, in measureless oceans of space,
Ceaselessly musing, venturing, throwing, seeking the spheres
    to connect them,
Till the bridge you will need to be form'd, till the ductile
    anchor hold,
Till the gossamer thread you fling catch somewhere,
    O my soul.

"A NOISELESS PATIENT SPIDER"

A SPIDER WEB

"Put the question to our ancestors,
    study what they learned from their ancestors.
For we're newcomers at this, with a lot to learn,
    and not too long to learn it.
So why not let the ancients teach you, tell you what's what,
    instruct you in what they knew from experience?
Can mighty pine trees grow tall without soil?
    Can luscious tomatoes flourish without water?
Blossoming flowers look great before they're cut or picked,
    but without soil or water they wither
    more quickly than grass.
That's what happens to all who forget God—
    all their hopes come to nothing.
They hang their life from one thin thread,
    they hitch their fate to a spider web.
One jiggle and the thread breaks,
    one jab and the web collapses."

JOB 8:8-14

HERE'S WHAT I WANT YOU TO DO

Lo, soul, seest thou not God's purpose from the first?
The earth to be spann'd, connected by network,
The races, neighbors, to marry and be given in marriage,
The oceans to be cross'd, the distant brought near,
The lands to be welded together.

A worship new I sing,
You captains, voyagers, explorers, yours,
You engineers, you architects, machinists, yours,
You, not for trade or transportation only,
But in God's name, or for thy sake O soul.

FROM "PASSAGE TO INDIA"

HERE'S WHAT I WANT YOU TO DO

In light of all this, here's what I want you to do.
    While I'm locked up here, a prisoner for the Master,

I want you to get out there and walk
    —better yet, run!—
    on the road God called you to travel.
I don't want any of you sitting around on your hands.
I don't want anyone strolling off,
    down some path that goes nowhere.
And mark that you do this with humility and discipline
    —not in fits and starts, but steadily,
    pouring yourselves out for each other in acts of love,
    alert at noticing differences and quick at mending fences.

EPHESIANS 4:1-3

TO THE ENDS OF THE WORLD

O we can wait no longer,
We too take ship O soul,
Joyous we too launch out on trackless seas,
Fearless for unknown shores on waves of ecstacy to sail,
Amid the wafting winds, (thou pressing me to thee, I thee
    to me, O soul,)
Caroling free, singing our song of God,
Chanting our chant of pleasant exploration.

With laugh and many a kiss,
(Let others deprecate, let others weep for sin,
    remorse, humiliation,)
O soul thou pleasest me, I thee.

Ah more than any priest O soul we too believe in God,
But with the mystery of God we dare not dally.

FROM "PASSAGE TO INDIA"

TO THE ENDS OF THE WORLD

Dear Theophilus, in the first volume of this book I wrote on everything that Jesus began to do and teach until the day he said good-bye to the apostles, the ones he had chosen through the Holy Spirit, and was taken up to heaven. After his death, he presented himself alive to them in many different settings over a period of forty days. In face-to-face meetings, he talked to them about things concerning the kingdom of God. As they met and ate meals together, he told them that they were on no account to leave Jerusalem but "must wait for what the Father promised: the promise you heard from me. John baptized in water; you will be baptized in the Holy Spirit. And soon."

When they were together for the last time they asked, "Master, are you going to restore the kingdom to Israel now? Is this the time?"

He told them, "You don't get to know the time. Timing is the Father's business. What you'll get is the Holy Spirit. And when the Holy Spirit comes on you, you will be able to be my witnesses in Jerusalem, all over Judea and Samaria, even to the ends of the world."

ACTS 1:1-8

THESE TEARS OF MINE

Whispers of heavenly death murmur'd I hear,
Labial gossip of night, sibilant chorals,
Footsteps gently ascending, mystical breezes wafted soft
    and low,
Ripples of unseen rivers, tides of a current flowing,
    forever flowing,
(Or is it the plashing of tears? the measureless waters of
    human tears?)

FROM "WHISPERS OF HEAVENLY DEATH"

THESE TEARS OF MINE

*"Ah, G*OD*, listen to my prayer, my*
    cry—open your ears.
Don't be callous;
    just look at these tears of mine.
I'm a stranger here. I don't know my way—
    a migrant like my whole family.
Give me a break, cut me some slack
    before it's too late and I'm out of here."

PSALM 39:12-13

LIVE GENEROUSLY

I saw the face of the most smear'd and slobbering idiot they
    had at the asylum,
And I knew for my consolation what they knew not,
I knew of the agents that emptied and broke my brother,
The same wait to clear the rubbish from the fallen tenement,
And I shall look again in a score or two of ages,
And I shall meet the real landlord perfect and unharm'd,
    every inch as good as myself.

FROM "FACES"

LIVE GENEROUSLY

The prayer was no sooner prayed than it was answered. Jesus called twelve of his followers and sent them into the ripe fields. He gave them power to kick out the evil spirits and to tenderly care for the bruised and hurt lives.... Jesus sent his twelve harvest hands out with this charge:

Don't begin by traveling to some far-off place
    to convert unbelievers.
Don't try to be dramatic by tackling some public enemy.
Go to the lost, confused people right here
    in the neighborhood.
Tell them that the kingdom is here.
Bring health to the sick.
Raise the dead.
Touch the untouchables.
Kick out the demons.

"You have been treated generously, so live generously."

MATTHEW 10:1, 5-8

QUIET POOLS TO DRINK FROM

Blow trumpeter free and clear, I follow thee,
While at thy liquid prelude, glad, serene,
The fretting world, the streets, the noisy hours
    of day withdraw,
A holy calm descends like dew upon me,
I walk in cool refreshing night the walks of Paradise,
I scent the grass, the moist air and the roses;
Thy song expands my numb'd imbonded spirit, thou freest,
    launchest me,
Floating and basking upon heaven's lake.

FROM "THE MYSTIC TRUMPETER"

QUIET POOLS TO DRINK FROM

God, my shepherd!
  I don't need a thing.
You have bedded me down in lush meadows,
    you find me quiet pools to drink from.
True to your word,
    you let me catch my breath
    and send me in the right direction.
Even when the way goes through
    Death Valley,
I'm not afraid
    when you walk at my side.
Your trusty shepherd's crook
    makes me feel secure.

PSALM 23:1-4

WHAT ARE YOU TALKING ABOUT?

Let the reformers descend from the stands where they are
forever bawling—let an idiot or insane person appear
on each of the stands;
Let judges and criminals be transposed—let the prison-
keepers be put in prison—let those that were prisoners
take the keys;
Let them that distrust birth and death lead the rest.

"TRANSPOSITIONS"

WHAT ARE YOU TALKING ABOUT?

"Then he will turn to the 'goats,' the ones on his left, and say, 'Get out, worthless goats! You're good for nothing but the fires of hell. And why? Because—

> *I was hungry and you gave me no meal,*
> *I was thirsty and you gave me no drink,*
> *I was homeless and you gave me no bed,*
> *I was shivering and you gave me no clothes,*
> *Sick and in prison, and you never visited.*

"Then those 'goats' are going to say, 'Master, what are you talking about? When did we ever see you hungry or thirsty or homeless or shivering or sick or in prison and didn't help?'

"He will answer them, 'I'm telling the solemn truth: Whenever you failed to do one of these things to someone who was being overlooked or ignored, that was me—you failed to do it to me.'

"Then those 'goats' will be herded to their eternal doom, but the 'sheep' to their eternal reward."

MATTHEW 25:41-46

INHERITANCE

As at thy portals also death,
Entering thy sovereign, dim, illimitable grounds,
To memories of my mother, to the divine blending,
        maternity,
To her, buried and gone, yet buried not, gone not from me,
(I see again the calm benignant face fresh and beautiful still,
I sit by the form in the coffin,
I kiss and kiss convulsively again the sweet old lips, the
        cheeks, the closed eyes in the coffin;)
To her, the ideal woman, practical, spiritual, of all of earth,
        life, love, to me the best,
I grave a monumental line, before I go, amid these songs,
And set a tombstone here.

"AS AT THY PORTALS ALSO DEATH"

INHERITANCE

When his mother died, Toby buried her next to his father. Then he and his wife, Sarah, and their children left for Media, where they would live with his father-in-law, Raguel, and mother-in-law, Edna, in Ecbatana.

Toby took good care of his in-laws, treating them with dignity and respect. Their final resting place was in their hometown.

According to the will of both his father and his father-in-law, Toby and Sarah received both inheritances.

TOBIT 14:12-13

BEND AN EAR, GOD!

A batter'd, wreck'd old man,
Thrown on this savage shore, far, far from home,
Pent by the sea and dark rebellious brows, twelve
    dreary months,
Sore, stiff with many toils, sicken'd and nigh to death,
I take my way along the island's edge,
Venting a heavy heart.

I am too full of woe!
Haply I may not live another day;
I cannot rest O God, I cannot eat or sleep,
Till I put forth myself, my prayer, once more to Thee,
Breathe, bathe myself once more in Thee, commune
    with Thee,
Report myself once more to Thee.

FROM "PRAYER OF COLUMBUS"

BEND AN EAR, GOD!

Bend an ear, GOD; answer me.
　　I'm one miserable wretch!
Keep me safe—haven't I lived a good life?
　　Help your servant—I'm depending on you!
You're my God; have mercy on me.
　　I count on you from morning to night.
Give your servant a happy life;
　　I put myself in your hands!
You're well-known as good and forgiving,
　　bighearted to all who ask for help.
Pay attention, GOD, to my prayer;
　　bend down and listen to my cry for help.
Every time I'm in trouble I call on you,
　　confident that you'll answer.

PSALM 86:1-7

WHY WE ARE HERE

Hast never come to thee an hour,
A sudden gleam divine, precipitating, bursting all these
      bubbles, fashions, wealth?
These eager business aims—books, politics, art, amours,
To utter nothingness?

"HAST NEVER COME TO THEE AN HOUR"

WHY WE ARE HERE

"Let me tell you why you are here. You're here to be salt-seasoning that brings out the God-flavors of this earth. If you lose your saltiness, how will people taste godliness? You've lost your usefulness and will end up in the garbage.

"Here's another way to put it: You're here to be light, bringing out the God-colors in the world. God is not a secret to be kept. We're going public with this, as public as a city on a hill. If I make you light-bearers, you don't think I'm going to hide you under a bucket, do you? I'm putting you on a light stand. Now that I've put you there on a hilltop, on a light stand—shine! Keep open house; be generous with your lives. By opening up to others, you'll prompt people to open up with God, this generous Father in heaven."

MATTHEW 5:13-16

A SOUP OF NOTHINGNESS

Spirit that form'd this scene,
These tumbled rock-piles grim and red,
These reckless heaven-ambitious peaks,
These gorges, turbulent-clear streams, this naked freshness,
These formless wild arrays, for reasons of their own,
I know thee, savage spirit—we have communed together,
Mine too such wild arrays, for reasons of their own;
Was't charged against my chants they had forgotten art?
To fuse within themselves its rules precise and delicatesse?
The lyrist's measur'd beat, the wrought-out temple's grace—
          column and polish'd arch forgot?
But thou that revelest here—spirit that form'd this scene,
They have remember'd thee.

"SPIRIT THAT FORM'D THIS SCENE"

A SOUP OF NOTHINGNESS

First this:

> God created the Heavens and Earth
>   —all you see, all you don't see.
> Earth was a soup of nothingness,
>   a bottomless emptiness,
>   an inky blackness.
> God's Spirit brooded like a bird
>   above the watery abyss.

GENESIS I:I-2

WHAT GOD WANTS

Gliding o'er all, through all,
Through Nature, Time, and Space,
As a ship on the waters advancing,
The voyage of the soul—not life alone,
Death, many deaths I'll sing.

"GLIDING O'ER ALL"

WHAT GOD WANTS

Don't love the world's ways.
Don't love the world's goods.
Love of the world squeezes out love
  for the Father.
Practically everything that goes on in
  the world—wanting your own way,
  wanting everything for yourself, wanting
  to appear important—has nothing to do
  with the Father. It just isolates
  you from him.
The world and all its wanting, wanting,
  wanting is on the way out—but whoever
  does what God wants is set for eternity.

I JOHN 2:15-17

ANALOGIES

As I watch'd the ploughman ploughing,
Or the sower sowing in the fields, or the harvester harvesting,
I saw there too, O life and death, your analogies;
(Life, life is the tillage, and Death is the harvest according.)

"AS I WATCH'D THE PLOUGHMAN PLOUGHING"

ANALOGIES

But the Melchizedek story provides a perfect analogy: Jesus, a priest like Melchizedek, not by genealogical descent but by the sheer force of resurrection life—he lives!—"priest forever in the royal order of Melchizedek." The former way of doing things, a system of commandments that never worked out the way it was supposed to, was set aside; the law brought nothing to maturity. Another way—Jesus!—a way that does *work, that brings us right into the presence of God, is put in its place.*

HEBREWS 7:15-19

BRAVO!

These carols sung to cheer my passage through the world
    I see.
For completion I dedicate to the Invisible World.

"THESE CAROLS"

BRAVO!

Bravo, GOD, Bravo!
Everyone join in the great shout: Encore!
In awe before the beauty, in awe before the might.
Bring gifts and celebrate,
Bow before the beauty of GOD,
Then to your knees—everyone worship!
Get out the message—GOD Rules!
He put the world on a firm foundation;
He treats everyone fair and square.
Let's hear it from Sky,
With Earth joining in,
And a huge round of applause from Sea.
Let Wilderness turn cartwheels,
Animals, come dance,
Put every tree of the forest in the choir—
An extravaganza before GOD as he comes,
As he comes to set everything right on earth,
Set everything right, treat everyone fair.

PSALM 96:7-13

ENTER THE SILENCE

After the dazzle of day is gone,
Only the dark, dark night shows to my eyes the stars;
After the clangor of organ majestic, or chorus,
    or perfect band,
Silent, athwart my soul, moves the symphony true.

"AFTER THE DAZZLE OF DAY"

ENTER THE SILENCE

When life is heavy and hard to take,
*   go off by yourself. Enter the silence.*
Bow in prayer. Don't ask questions:
*   Wait for hope to appear.*
Don't run from trouble. Take it full-face.
*   The "worst" is never the worst.*

LAMENTATIONS 3:28-30

ENTER THE MYSTERY

Good-bye my Fancy!
Farewell dear mate, dear love!
I'm going away, I know not where,
Or to what fortune, or whether I may ever see you again,
So Good-bye my Fancy.

Now for my last—let me look back a moment;
The slower fainter ticking of he clock is in me,
Exit, nightfall, and soon the heart-thud stopping.

Long have we lived, joy'd, carress'd together;
Delightful!—now separation—Good-bye my Fancy.

Yet let me not be too hasty,
Long indeed have we lived, slept, filter'd, become really
    blended into one;
Then if we die we die together, (yes, we'll remain one,)
If we go anywhere we'll go together to meet what happens,
May-be we'll be better off and blither, and learn something,
May-be it is yourself now really ushering me to the true
    songs, (who knows?)
May-be it is you the mortal knob really undoing, turning—
    so now finally,
Good-bye—and hail! my Fancy.

"GOOD-BYE, MY FANCY!"

112

ENTER THE MYSTERY

I waited and waited and waited for GOD.
    At last he looked; finally he listened.
He lifted me out of the ditch,
    pulled me from deep mud.
He stood me up on a solid rock
    to make sure I wouldn't slip.
He taught me how to sing the latest God-song,
    a praise-song to our God.
More and more people are seeing this:
    they enter the mystery,
    abandoning themselves to GOD.

PSALM 40:1-3

LIMITS TO EVERYTHING HUMAN

This is the hour O soul, thy free flight into the wordless,
Away from books, away from art, the day erased,
    the lesson done,
Thee fully forth emerging, silent, gazing, pondering the
    themes thou lovest best,
Night, sleep, death and the stars.

"A CLEAR MIDNIGHT"

LIMITS TO EVERYTHING HUMAN

What you say goes, GOD,
*   and stays, as permanent as the heavens.*
Your truth never goes out of fashion;
*   it's as up-to-date as the earth when the sun comes up.*
Your Word and truth are dependable as ever;
*   that's what you ordered—you set the earth going.*
If your revelation hadn't delighted me so,
*   I would have given up when the hard times came.*
But I'll never forget the advice you gave me;
*   you saved my life with those wise words.*
Save me! I'm all yours.
*   I look high and low for your words of wisdom.*
The wicked lie in ambush to destroy me,
*   but I'm only concerned with your plans for me.*
I see the limits to everything human,
*   but the horizons can't contain your commands!*

PSALM 119:89-96

115

INDEX OF POEMS

SCRIPTURE INDEX

Norbert Krapf, former Indiana Poet Laureate, taught English for over 30 years at Long Island University, where he directed the C.W. Post Poetry Center. He holds a BA in English from St. Joseph's College (IN) and an MA and PhD in English and American literature from the University of Notre Dame. He was a Fulbright Professor of American Poetry at the Universities of Freiburg and Erlangen-Nuremberg in Germany. The most recent of his twenty-seven books are the poetry collection *Catholic Boy Blues: A Poet's Journal of Healing*, and the prose memoir *Shrinking the Monster: Healing the Wounds of Our Abuse*, winner of an Illumination Book Award. He has won the Lucille Medwick Memorial Award from the Poetry Society of America, a Glick Indiana Author Award for the body of his work, and a Creative Renewal Fellowship from the Arts Council of Indianapolis. Walt Whitman and bluesman Robert Johnson inspired him to begin writing poetry in 1971. Norbert has collaborated with jazz pianist-composer Monika Herzig and bluesman Gordon Bonham. For more, see www.krapfpoetry.com.